F

MW00831918

VALUABLE

"How can we find honest love when we haven't been honest with how we feel about ourselves? *She's Valuable (But Does She Know It?)* is a must read for all women who desire something real! As a woman who's action's reflect her true worth, Dominique's real approach to manifesting a lasting relationship by first loving yourself is the perfect "how to" and refresher tool all wrapped in one powerful message that every woman needs to hear, YOU'RE VALUABLE!"

– Paul Carrick Brunson,
Founder of the Paul Carrick Brunson Agency
and Host of Our World TV

"DClark has always provided REAL advice about love and relationships that is both positive and relatable to all women. That is why I am excited about this book that truly touches on self-love and identity, something that many women deal with on a day-to-day basis. So, whether you are having an identity crisis in a relationship or your identity crisis is keeping you from being in a relationship or you just love to read uplifting books, then *She's Valuable (But Does She Know It?)* is for you!"

– London Alexaundria,
Managing Editor of *SHEEN* Magazine

"Dominique turns the challenges of dating into a fun and exciting journey. Her personality is so magnetic and every conversation with Dominique offers compassion, wisdom and great advice. After one conversation with her you feel uplifted and confident. Her daily practice is a shining example of everything she preaches.

She is the girl that makes you think, *Where have you been all my life?* She is the girlfriend everyone needs!"

– Alex Butler,
Host of My Carolina Today on NBC

She's
VALUABLE

She's
VALUABLE
But Does She Know It?

DOMINIQUE
CLARK

FOREWORD BY PAUL CARRICK BRUNSON

Tandem Light Press

Tandem Light Press
950 Herrington Rd.
Suite C128
Lawrenceville, GA 30044

Tandem Light Press paperback edition August 2016

ISBN: 9780997229622
Library of Congress Control Number: 2016941734

Biblical passages are from the King James Bible

PRINTED IN THE UNITED STATES OF AMERICA

To my sweet girls, Zoë Drew and Zara Rae, may you always know the incomparable beauty that lies within each of you. Mommy loves you more than you could ever think and I pray every word of this book and every day of my life makes you proud to be an extension of me. You are my joy!

Your crown is not invisible…
– Dominique Clark

CONTENTS

FOREWORD

Ladies, it is with great pleasure that I inform you of the power you now hold in your hands. If you are willing to take this transformational journey, this book will create a defining moment on how you look at yourself, men, and relationships.

Dominique has brought to life the truth about what's holding so many of you incredible women back from experiencing the love you truly desire. It's complicated (but it doesn't have to be), so she shares with you a very simple and easy to grasp concept that will put you on the path to relationship success, starting with yourself. Implementing the guidelines outlined in this book with her own clients and witnessing their consistent change and accomplishment over the years gives me the confidence to join this movement.

Dominique and I were initially introduced some years ago on twitter. She was new to the matchmaking industry and wanted to connect and learn from someone who not only looked like her, but who had also found success in the areas she aspired. I was several episodes in on a platform I created to offer mentorship from myself and other influencers and thought leaders to the masses, called Mentor Monday, so I was enthusiastic about responding to Dominique's tweets about starting and branding DClark & Company.

I knew she was serious about perfecting her craft and being a true influencer in the relationship space when we met in person for the first time in New York at a Matchmaker's Conference. Her desire and passion to have a substantial impact as a matchmaker and coach lead me to offer her an internship opportunity with my company, The Paul Brunson Agency. She did an awesome job! At the start of her internship, I asked Dominique one question:

"What problem are you solving? There are tons of 'experts' out there, what's going to separate you from the pack?" I wanted her to really establish herself and get specific about what her personal and professional experiences will uniquely offer singles. That's why it's so amazing that this book is all about understanding your value. That's exactly what I challenged her to do in a professional sense, and she did just that, and know she's challenging you on a personal level.

Life is not a dress rehearsal; this is it! Dominique does a great job at transparently showing you, through snippets of her personal story and that of other women, how communicating and owning your value right now is the ultimate transition from experiencing potentially good relationships to stepping into your dream relationship. It's all in the preparation and being ready when that moment arrives. It takes strength and a willingness to grow, and Dominique is the ultimate accountability partner to see you through! Her passion for improving the quality of lives through love and relationship is undeniable.

This is a book for those who dare to ask, "Why me?" for women who are not afraid to face themselves and own their truth. It's that "get it together" slap on the hands you need with a positive push and actionable steps. This book helps you unveil the number one reason possibly holding you back from love: YOU!

How can we find honest love when we haven't been honest with how we feel about ourselves? *She's Valuable (But Does She Know It?)* is a must read for all women who desire something real! As a woman whose action's reflect her true worth, Dominique's real approach to manifesting a lasting relationship by first loving yourself is the perfect "how to" and refresher tool all wrapped in one powerful message that every woman needs to hear, YOU'RE VALUABLE!

- Paul Carrick Brunson

PREFACE

So, I'm sure you're probably thinking, "Why is a matchmaker writing a book about worth and not about love?" Believe it or not I was actually thinking the same thing when God initially put this topic on my heart. I just knew my first book would cover "Dating 101," "Finding the Perfect Match" or "How to Find a Guy in 10 Days and Keep Him"! Much easier topics to approach with my line of work, and can be a much lighter conversation to have, right?

But after much thought on why I just couldn't get around addressing a woman's worth from a matchmaker's perspective, it was clear that this conversation had to happen first before we could ever talk about being the perfect mate or even attracting one for that matter. Ladies, knowing your value and understanding your worth is a prerequisite to true love. Want to find something real and keep it? The number one quality you must display and possess is self-worth!

So, how do you know if you really know your own worth, anyway? Maybe you feel like you've always had a positive perception of your value, but could use a reminder, maybe you feel like you're not valuable at all and need to rebuild from the bottom up or you could even find yourself smack dab in the middle and benefit from an empowering refresher because you're now questioning it.

Wherever you find yourself, you've got to identify your baseline! Take my Value Assessment now, before reading the book, and discover how you perceive your value, then take it again after reading the book to track your progress. Whether your results are good or not so good, remember that this is a process that doesn't happen overnight, but I believe in you and I'm certainly here with you as your accountability partner every step of the way! And hey! You've already taken the first step by purchasing this book, so you're ahead of the game! Let's Go!

VALUE ASSESSMENT

1. a) I'm a gift and my existence matters.
    b) There's nothing special about me. The world would go on whether I was here or not.

2. a) I deserve the best and never settle for anything less.
    b) I accept the cards dealt to me because deep inside I don't believe I deserve more.

3. a) I have great work-life balance. The people that I date treat me with the upmost respect.
    b) I have excelled in my career, but when it comes to relationships, I have a habit of dating douche bags.

4. a) I am blessed with an authentic friendship circle and attract positive people in my life.

b) I'm surrounded by negative people who make more withdrawals from my life than deposits.

5. a) I love myself and know that I don't need to be perfect.
   b) It's hard to find things to love about myself.

6. a) I'm positive and look for the good in every situation.
   b) I worry a lot and feel like things never work out for my good.

7. a) I've never been so desperate for love that I've allowed a man to devalue me.
   b) I've allowed men to not treat me in the manner in which I'm worth and have made excuses for their actions.

8. a) I don't spend any time comparing myself to other women.
   b) I find it difficult to be self-focused without measuring myself to other women.

9. a) Society's idea of what makes a woman valuable has no reflection on how I feel about myself.
   b) I often find myself trying to keep up with today's standard of beauty.

10. a) It makes me feel good when someone gives me a compliment.
    b) It's hard for me to take a compliment because I don't always believe it.

11. a) If a great guy approached me and expressed interest I have no problem flirting with him.
    b) If a great guy approached me and expressed interest, I subconsciously find a way to sabotage it or don't even recognize he's interested at all.

12. a) I'm Valuable!
    b) I'm still trying to discover my worth.

VALUE ASSESSMENT SCORING SYSTEM

All done? Great! Tally up your number of "b" responses and let's see how you did:

B = 8-12: SHE's Valuable, but doesn't know it! Read every word of this book and trust the process! I believe in you! You're worthy!

B = 4-8: SHE's Valuable but isn't fully confident in who she is yet, so completely loving herself is a challenge. You can do this! Know that you're a gift!

B = 0-4: SHE's Valuable but has moments of questioning it, and it's okay! We've all been there! But now it's time to really believe it!

B = 0: Congrats! SHE's Valuable and you OWN it with every fiber of your being! Read this book and keep it in your arsenal as the ultimate reminder and refresher tool.

ACKNOWLEDGMENTS

There's no better place to begin than with God! I'm so thankful that I was obedient to his will for my life, even when I doubted the process at times. To entrust me with servicing his people in this way is a blessing and I don't take it for granted! I am forever grateful for his presence and unfailing direction.

To my amazing husband, Wesley Clark, aka "Wes the Best"! I thank you so much for your patience and sacrificial spirit. You are my rock! Thank you for loving me on purpose. Your support and understanding as I carry out my dreams is unwavering and I'm truly blessed for that. Who knew we would be the high school sweethearts that made it? I love you to the moon and back. Blessed to be your wife is an understatement!

To my amazing and beautiful daughters Zoë Drew Clark and Zara Rae Clark, mommy thanks you for choosing me! I thank you for being my greatest motivation and greatest accomplishments! Your spirits lift me! I love you!

To my phenomenal mother, Linda Rogers-Brown. Not sure that I could thank you enough! I appreciate your push, your drive, sacrifice, and the incredible example you are of a woman, wife, mother, and entrepreneur. You've been my greatest teacher and one of the greatest blessings in my life. My love for you is eternal. I AM because YOU ARE!

To my father Alfred Rogers, I thank you for believing in me, being proud of me, and investing in a personal relationship with me! I'm beyond grateful for your continued support and presence in my life.

To my grandmother Hattie May, I thank you and love you so much! I delight in your humor and embody your strength.

To my talented sister Kimberly Davis! Thank you for giving me the initial push and encouragement to pursue my passions. I love you!

To my sister and brother cousins Lakai and Kevin Vinson, thank you for being an incredible example and inspiration to me and my family. I love you!

To my sister Linda Rambert, thank you for always believing in me and always challenging me to be greater!

To my best friend Mrs., Margarete Neely, thank you for giving me balance and loving me as if I were your own. I am grateful for your life and the influence you've had on mine! Love you!

To my business coach Thomas Calhoun, thank you for being my EVERYTHING coach and brother from another. I am grateful for your continued belief and confidence in my purpose! You challenge me to stretch.

To my author coach Caroline, thank you for being my accountability partner and guiding light throughout this process of creating something I am so proud of! You're the best sister–friend–author coach I know!

To all my family, dear friends, spiritual and business mentors, I'm blessed to have you! Thank you for being positive supporters, motivators, prayer partners, and advisors in my life! I wouldn't trade you!

INTRODUCTION

As a Professional Matchmaker and Relationship Coach, I provide personal matchmaking and dating coaching for professional singles, relationship enhancement experiences for couples, and image consulting for all who are looking to revamp their style! Being a part of such an industry grants me the luxury of meeting so many amazing people who are willing to share their journeys with me, and who trust me to help them discover a solution to their relationship challenges. I don't take that lightly! I get the privilege of being a part of their growth, their love stories, but most importantly, an intimate and private space that many are not so openly invited.

As you can probably imagine, my office is constantly flooded with incredible women in pursuit of trying to find the perfect guy. They all feel that they've either exhausted all their abilities to find the perfect men, or they believe that those men just don't exist anymore. These are both valid concerns, but the number one problem I find with women is not in that they can't find the right guy, it's that they are looking for men who are not necessarily looking for them! Most of the time women are dating by default; they haven't identified what they really need in a relationship, so they have no idea who or what they should be looking for. Furthermore, because of adverse internal and or external sways, many women have failed to recognize their own significance. This is a direct reflection of not truly knowing, owning, and loving who you are.

Before the matchmaking or coaching process begins, I start with a consultation to learn about potential clients — their challenges, their relationship goals, and what they're looking for in a partner. The first question I ask both women and men during their consultation with me is: "Why you? What makes you valuable? What value will you add to a relationship?" The majority of the men have no problem quickly and assertively answering this question. The ladies, on the other hand, not so much. The first response I typically receive from women is something like "Wow, that's a good question…let me think about that." Instinctually, they begin to run down the list of all their accolades and accomplishments, or physical features that they feel are appealing to men. I sit back and watch them take a moment to dig through their memory bank of all the compliments anyone had ever paid them, as opposed to the praises that come from them just thinking highly of themselves for who they are.

The problem that I've found is that none of these women knew what truly made them valuable or they had barely scratched the surface! No one says it's my intelligence, my integrity, my humanity, my values! They barely speak about the things that truly matter. So, I can always count on my first session or assignment for them being identifying what makes them great and an ideal match for a man.

The idea of worth and value got me thinking that this is not only an issue for the single women who walk through my door, but also for the billions of women—from teenagers to co-eds to grandmothers—across the world who don't know their worth and have difficulty discovering it...those who've allowed society or challenging past experiences to define it for them!

As my thoughts deepened I thought about the women who face cultural constraints, who are victims of rape (like myself), suffered from abuse, and continued beyond the expiration date from one dysfunctional relationship to the next. Women who feel powerless and, for some, can only manage to control one thing, and that's their ability to learn, get an education and develop professionally. It's one thing that no one can take away from them and the single thread keeping them from drowning in a sea of complete worthlessness.

In an effort to put a dent in this problem, I felt lead to start the SHE's Valuable Movement, a movement that stands on Proverbs 3:15 "She is more precious than rubies, and all the things you may desire can compare with her," and Proverbs 31:10 "...her worth is far above rubies."

The goal of this movement is to empower women all over our nation, especially young professionals and those in the college space, to identify and own what makes them valuable; to encourage these women to share their worth with the world, especially with men, in order to break the cycles that perpetuate this epidemic!

1

JUDGING MYSELF THROUGH SOMEONE ELSE'S EYES

...she is far more precious than jewels and her value is far above rubies.
–Proverbs 31:10

Have you ever heard of a mastermind group? If so, maybe you've had the opportunity to participate in one. Well, for those who are unfamiliar, a mastermind group provides an opportunity for people to brainstorm, educate and support each other around a particular idea and promote growth. I conducted a series of mastermind groups that consisted of professional women—primarily between the ages of twenty-five and thirty-five—to collect data in preparation for writing this book. As you probably already guessed, the idea discussed was our ability as women to identity our self-worth and the challenges associated with it. Each woman courageously shared her story as the other members of the group supported her through. There were a lot of: "Girl, me too! And "I've been there before." It was truly a shared endeavor for all. We had many moments of laughter and a few where we cried, but it was an enlightening experience to say the least.

What I'm about to share with you next, and throughout the remainder of this book are pieces from some of their stories that are identifiable and demonstrate how we as women can be stripped of our value and the necessary steps to reclaim it, starting with myself!

From the outside looking in, my appearance, my style of dress, the way I wear my hair, the way I walk confidently into a room or the fact that I smile until there is no end may have many thinking, "Wow, this girl has it together!" I've even been told that I have an "X factor," or should I say je ne sais quoi! But, have you ever heard of the phrase "Fake It Till You Make It"? Sure you have! Well it makes sense on some levels, but in actuality, it's simply bad advice. It was meant to encourage people who lacked confidence or bravery in a certain area, to lead with their actions instead of their feelings and then their feelings would soon follow suit. With that being said, I had to do a lot of "faking" before I truly realized and believed in the value of the woman I am today! I couldn't live life to my fullest potential without an understanding of my worth. I couldn't maintain good relationships with others—whether intimate, business, or casual friendships—because I was caught in a web of self-doubt, low self-esteem, and uncertainty. But once I was aware that my uniqueness was my gift, and that I was truly just as valuable as everyone else, I wholeheartedly began to live!

Before I was tainted by the categories, or should I say "standards" of beauty society has so nicely created for women, I was this confident, goofy, and tomboy-ish little girl without a care in the world! I had no pressure to be accepted and had no fear of judgment. I was an athlete, so most of the time I wore sneakers and comfortable clothing, and reserved the frilly dresses for church on Sunday mornings. I had good friends with no agendas, no cattiness, competiveness, or comparisons — just good friends. I could play dolls with the girls and basketball with the guys and everything was just fine! I wore my hair in a curly afro puff, slicked back with water and Blue Magic hair grease, tied together with my favorite scrunchie! And, sometimes, on special occasions my mom would put individual twists in my hair with colorful rubber bands like rapper, Da Brat! Again, everything was just fine!

I entered middle school, and on the first day of class, my world was forever changed. For the first time in my life I felt uncomfortable in my own skin. My male peers became the guys looking to check me (and not like in the game of basketball), and I quickly fell out of the running to be "liked," "crushed on," or any of those kidlike phrases we used to use growing up. See, I didn't meet the mark. I didn't have relaxed hair hanging to my shoulders fresh out of a wrap, light skin, "girly" apparel, budding breasts, or a big ole butt. That was the standard then. I was just a kid! And suddenly I felt pressured to be something else. In an instant, I had unknowingly given my middle school peers the power to determine my worth. My mom and dad told me I was pretty and perfect, but as parents, they are obligated to do that, right? Their opinions fell on deaf ears because those at school mattered more. They had such a profound effect on me in just one day, that I went home and immediately asked my mom to take out the twists in my hair she had spent hours on the night before. It was only right…right?

As I was trying to determine where I "fit" and why my body wasn't reacting to graduating from fifth grade like the other girls, I found myself highly infatuated with this guy! Everyone had a "crush" and some even progressed to boyfriend and girlfriend, and I wanted to be next in line! We both played sports, we were the same height, and he was super cute! Match made in heaven, right? So one day I saw him getting ready to approach me. I was nervous and excited all at the same time. He walked over to me with this great smile and I thought: wow maybe he likes me too! We were standing face to face and he extended his hands out to give me the popular "dap greeting" and we shook hands. He frowned while he said "Ouch, your hands feel like sandpaper!" Everyone surrounding us began to laugh and that was the first time I felt unworthy. That one experience has stuck with me since then. From that moment on, I have always been self-conscious about shaking someone's hand, so for a long time, I wouldn't do it! Instead I would say, "I'm a hugger" and offer a hug instead. While at church when the pastor would instruct the congregation to "grab your neighbor's hand" for prayer, I would get so much anxiety from the thought of not knowing what the person next to me was thinking about my hands that I would miss the entire content of the prayer. Crazy, right? That experience, which may seem minor to others, made me believe that no man could ever want me. Men like women with soft hands, and I didn't have them. How could I be valuable? (Today, I'm thankful for my husband who loves me regardless of whether I have soft hands or not.)

Life is all about perception. Your worth is based on how people perceive you, and suddenly how you present yourself and all the superficial details of who you are become very important. This became even truer to me when I entered high school. I didn't always have the latest style of clothing or belong to a popular group of girlfriends, but I did manage talk my mother into getting my hair done professionally for the first time so that I could wear my hair relaxed and wrapped like the rest of the popular girls! I felt the need to be validated by others. Sadly, I lived for compliments (especially from men...and this continued into adulthood) and for popular kids to speak and hold a conversation with me! I felt "cool" when this happened. I loved it when guys would flirt with me because I felt pretty and thought that each compliment or moment of acceptance would add back a layer of value that I felt was taken away from me back in middle school. I had attached my self-worth to the perception of what others thought of me. Thankfully, this didn't last very long. The thought of constantly needing to look the part, act tough and unbothered and get the hottest guy was exhausting. I couldn't understand why girls felt the need to do this, or why I was even attempting, but through my actions, I would try to "fake it" with hopes of making it! Eventually, my feelings began to conquer my actions. When my actions were no longer enough, God would bring me right back to the girl he created me to be! Not who my peers said I should be. And although I may have been alone, or not always amongst the popular kids, I was okay. I was so young, yet still understood the power of God and believed in his words. He said, "She is far more precious than jewels and her value is far above rubies," and that comforted me.

God isolated me for a reason. I wasn't supposed to be seen by everyone or be liked by everyone. He was preparing me and setting the stage for a connection that would change my sensitivity moving forward. It wasn't until I met a new guy that the perception I had of myself really changed. Crazy, how we can all fall victim to a good-looking guy edifying us. We were in the same Civics class in ninth grade, and we both sat in the back of the room. I noticed that he would flirt with me frequently in class, but I would often question if it was because he really liked me, or if he had ulterior motives (he was a basketball player, and could probably date any other girl besides me). He was a popular guy; a nice guy who was very funny! He was always the mastermind of every joke and loved basketball. I would think, *why me? What could he possibly see in me?* Much later, I realized that he wasn't interested in me because I compared to the other more stylish and popular girls, or because he was looking for any sexual favors. He was interested in me because of the very thing that made me valuable. I was a young lady of integrity, I had a standard, I saw the significance in developing a friendship, and cared about who he was as a person. My physical features where just the icing on the cake.

The Power of Childhood

> *Your character – your nature, the distinctive qualities of your essence, what make you – is developed through experience. When life detects that there is an opportunity for you to advance the nature of your character, it will send the perfect situation and people your way. Your job is to respond in a manner that develops and strengthens your character.*
>
> - Iyanla Vanzant

Don't you just love sunny days with cool breezes? There's something about days like this that eagerly force you out of your house with no agenda at all, just so you can experience the fullness of beauty it has to offer! I remember one particular day like this that lured me downtown in the city I lived in for some of the best ice cream in the area, in my opinion, from a cute little pink shop called the Parlour! As I carelessly approached the never-ending line to ice cream heaven, I noticed a range of cracks along the pavement sidewalk that immediately triggered a childhood memory of me at six years old with my neighborhood friends. We were playing hopscotch on the sidewalk, each rectangle block outlined with our favorite color chalk. As we played, we would often toss in another challenge by chanting the saying: "Step on a crack and break your mother's back." Reminiscing about this, I laughed a little out loud as I found my place in line strategically avoiding all the cracks along the way.

It's amazing how influential our childhood experiences are on our adult lives. They affect our decision-making, the way we perceive ourselves, and how we relate to others. Good or bad, all it takes is one smell, one song, one person or simply one crack in the pavement to take us back to a particular moment in time where we remember exactly how we felt, what we were wearing, the people involved and the details of the scenery. These experiences have an incredible ability to shift our emotions to happy or sad, doubtful or confident, and even if we've found a way to block them out of our memory, they'll never be erased from our DNA.

During the mastermind sessions I mentioned to you earlier, I asked each person to share the first experience they ever had that made them question their value. I wanted them to take a trip down memory lane, which many aren't so willing and don't find easy to do. Although the responses varied to the multitude of questions asked, there were a handful of women who recalled a childhood experience that transformed their once positive image of self to one of insignificance.

The story I will share with you in the next chapter is so important because there are so many of us whose self-worth is tarnished before we are old enough to even know what it is. In Chapter two, I will introduce you to *Bleached Skin and Empty Pockets*.

RECLAIM YOUR VALUE!

So, what about you? Have you found it difficult to look at yourself and know that you are valuable and enough? Have you ever really taken the lens off others and thought about your own amazing qualities? Take the next thirty minutes and only focus on yourself. Search deep, while also recognizing what may seem like insignificant assets, and dare to uncover them in the following space. Write down what you think makes you valuable and why.

2

BLEACHED SKIN & EMPTY POCKETS

It's never too late to be what you might have been.
–George Eliot

One of the most amazing, interesting, and inspiring women to ever walk this earth — a mentor in my head, and a prime example of a woman knowing and owning her worth — was Maya Angelou. She taught us all a thing or two about being a woman, slapped the back of our hands a few times with her life lessons, but uplifted us with her empowering and thought provoking words! She motivated us all to be more, to be strong! A strong woman, according to Maya, "...may encounter many defeats, but you must not be defeated. In fact, it may be necessary to encounter the defeats, so you can know who you are, what you can rise from, how you can still come out of it."

See, a weak woman is not aware of her strengths, her abilities, her power, her purpose. She is unable to lead and have an impact on a generation that so desperately needs her. When you are unable to define that which makes you valuable, when you are drifting on the opinions and validations of others, when you are unable to clearly see the gifts and talent waiting to erupt from the depths of your soul, you my dear, are not living, but instead drowning your life with emptiness.

So, how do you then define a valuable woman? What qualities does she possess? Well, a valuable girl, young lady, and woman is worthy of respect, admiration, and esteem. She is wise in her thinking, in her actions, and with her words. She diligently works for her family and in her purpose, and is an example to her peers; a valuable woman acknowledges a higher power and is centered on its truth.

The truth is, to be all these things can be really difficult for any woman living in today's society. Let's be honest, the social pressures of being a woman today are undeniable! From the workplace to keeping up with the newest trend that being a woman enforces, we can sometimes find ourselves lost on what's actually important. Now, don't get me wrong, men have their fair share of pressures too, like being strong and powerful, self-reliant and always in control. But for the purposes of this book, I'd like to highlight what most women encounter every day.

1. Being one kind of beautiful: long hair, thin waist, curvy exposed assets, perfect, symmetrical face, and dare I say big booty...

2. Sex Symbol

3. Perfect wife who maintains the house, cooks, does the laundry, nurtures the kids, etc.

4. Contributes financially to the household

5. Intelligent and holding our own, but not so established that we intimidate men

This list can go on and on! Now, I will say that some women naturally do these things, and do them well, but it's definitely a balancing act for the majority.

For me, being a wife, a mother, a friend, a sister, a churchgoer, business owner, daughter, mentor, author and a host of other things, it seems mind blowing that I manage to keep up with it all. I do the best that I can! But being a woman who knows her value and understanding that others look to my strength and abilities as motivation, I push through.

Bleached Skin and Empty Pockets

One very spirited and unfiltered woman, who for the sake of confidentiality we'll refer to as *Bleached Skin and Empty Pockets,* was very candid about a childhood experience that shifted her perspective of self and the type of person she thought she needed to be in order for anyone to see value in her.

Bleached Skin and Empty Pockets was a very talented and active child growing up. She was an athlete, volunteer, and honor roll student with a bright future ahead of her. To outsiders it appeared as if she came from a very stable family unit, but the truth was that she lived a very different reality at home. She had two parents at home who were married for years, but had a very interesting dichotomy. Her father was (and still is) a minister preaching the gospel and leading people to Christ, and her mother was a drug addict fighting to recover. *Bleached Skin and Empty Pockets* was ashamed of this truth and wanted no association with it.

Attending predominantly white schools growing up and observing the positive acknowledgments those within the white community received, and assuming that none of the other white children shared the same experience of having a mother battling an addiction, she felt devalued because of the color of her skin. She no longer saw value in being an African American woman. While at home, her mind would only allow her to see a black woman who selfishly chose the recreation of drugs over being a mother. She was angry that she couldn't just focus on being a kid and experience the excitement of looking to her mom in the stands rooting for her and supporting her at her basketball games. Instead, she hoped her mother didn't show at all to save her the embarrassment. Their roles were reversed. She was forced to be an adult who had to care for and try to support her mother through an addiction. She resented her mother and no longer wanted to identify herself with her. Because she couldn't see any value in the woman her mother was at the time, she couldn't see any value in herself. To appear as someone she was not, someone she thought others would respect and hold at high esteem, she attempted to bleach her skin, but was unsuccessful. Although she didn't verbally expand on the emotional and physical damage she endured as a result of this, the expression on her face and regretful tone of voice spoke loud and clear of that pain. She was willing to do anything to see someone other than her mother when she looked in the mirror.

In order to meet the expense of her addiction, her mother would find discreet ways of taking money from the family. Not only did *Bleached Skin and Empty Pockets* feel like she had to protect her self-image, but now she also had to protect her pockets. Her mother would cut their pants pockets to collect loose change. She hated this, but no matter how much she tried, she couldn't bleach her skin enough or predict which night her mother would go searching her pants pockets for money.

At the time, her mother didn't understand her power or worth beyond the drugs and had no sight of the movement she would later create to empower women because of it. So as a girl learning from her mother, it was hard for her to identify and realize her own power. As she got older, she had to learn that this experience was another chapter of her story and one of the driving forces that pushed her to strive for greater. The same strength and determination she developed to avoid association with her mother's challenges was the same strength and determination she needed to pour into her mother to support eradicating her mother's challenges.

Today she is a proud daughter who wholeheartedly loves and supports her mother! She now looks at that time as one that strengthened their mother-daughter relationship, and she stands delighted knowing that her reflection is the resemblance of someone she truly admires, loves, and can celebrate being clean for years to date. Although Bleached Skin and Empty Pockets couldn't see it at the time, her value lies in her stability and her ability to be a positive resource to those around her. She had to transform her mindset completely in order to understand that.

Now, as a mother herself, it's so important to her to understand and live her own value and worth for the sake of her two beautiful little girls. She makes it her duty to ensure that her daughters learn their value as women from her as their mother, and not from another woman of a different race or class, and certainly not from society.

Sometimes we have to see our pasts as a blessing for two reasons: 1) we are no longer there and 2) we've endured it. We need to analyze it and figure out the lessons meant to mold us and the experiences meant to grow us. We have to look back at those moments and say "Wow, I'm a strong somebody to have survived that!" It's all a matter of perception. And then when we experience that trigger that takes us back to what we use to describe as a hurtful moment, let it remind us of our strength instead, strength we can now use to conquer any other challenge life wants to through our way.

RECLAIM YOUR VALUE!

Take Action:

1. Think about the moment you first questioned your value. Was it within a relationship, challenges with your female counterparts or a familial experience? Identify the person or event in your past that has shattered your self-worth. Write it down!

_____

_____

_____

_____

2. Get Some Perspective: Try to get a clear understanding of why you experienced this and if it was something you even had control over. When your perspective becomes distorted, it's often because you've allowed the stressors from your past to drift into negative thinking and steal your joy. Before you know it, you stop appreciating your friends and family and doubt that they were ever for you. All of a sudden, the whole world is against you seemingly small issues become tremendously large, and you find yourself living in a world of worry and frustration.

A key to rising above the adversities of your past and gaining a positive perspective is finding things to be thankful for! In the space below, make a list! Write down all the good things and people in your life. Even though you can't always avoid negative circumstances, you can CHOOSE to focus on the positive and be happy with where you are and what you've been given.

_____

_____

_____

_____

3. Talk about it! Find someone you trust that can help you understand it better, sort through your emotions and give you comfort. Getting it off your chest is one of the best ways to lift the burden.

_____

_____

_____

_____

RECLAIM YOUR VALUE!

Mantra Moment

I've created several Mantra Moments throughout this book because I believe in speaking life and affirming yourself and the power it has over your perspective and your thoughts of the future. Write these mantras down on your favorite color post-it note, place it on your bathroom mirror and recite them as soon as you wake up each morning and before bed each night. Be sure to reflect on what they actually mean and believe it!

- I am valuable.
- "I am a woman. I am smart. I have opinions, I have feelings. I care. I make a difference. I matter. I am a woman and I am proud of who I am." – Unknown
- Not one drop of my self-worth depends on your acceptance of me.

When to use: When your past identity tries to define your present or future self. Use this to confirm your importance and value.

3

FATHERLESS DAUGHTER

[You are] a treasured daughter of our Heavenly father with
infinite worth.
– Dieter F. Uchtdorf

Every girl cherishes her father. Her father is her first love, her protector, and one of the most influential people in her life. His influence shapes her self-esteem, self-image, confidence, and opinions of men. Being called daddy's little girl can bring a girl so much joy and truly make her feel special and loved. But what happens when the man you're supposed to call daddy is inconsistent, no longer present or has never been present, whether physically or emotionally? What do you do when his exiting your life causes a ripple effect in the men you'd encounter in your adult life – repeatedly being left by men, not knowing why, and as a result questioning your value and producing self-doubt.

Where we place our value has a strong influence on our emotional stability. And for every young girl, she looks to her father to confirm her value, for it is the impact that fathers have on their lives that develops them into strong, confident women. Verbal encouragement, being consistently present in our life, being alert and sensitive to our feelings, taking time to listen to our thoughts, and taking an active interest in our hobbies, is the direct involvement and encouragement by our fathers that will help diminish a girl's insecurity and increase her confidence in her own abilities.

Many can strongly relate to the young lady who inspired this chapter in so many ways. *Fatherless Daughter,* a successful college student, experienced her father as an active part of her childhood, but when she became a young adult he was no longer in the picture. She loved her father, and with his exit, he created such a tremendous void leaving her to believe that she was the cause of his departure. She believed that it was her fault that he was no longer apart of her life, and because of that maybe she was unlovable – because you don't abandon someone you love, right? She began to experience this "one day you're in and the next you're out" sequence with the guys she would date.

Fatherless Daughter said, "They love me at first, but I'm not good enough for them to stay." What an incredible, yet heart wrenching revelation to have at such a young age. The magnitude of this thought became her belief and since she had unknowingly declared this in her life by speaking it, it had become her reality.

Fathers teach daughters boundaries and set standards that say, "you deserve better." So, what happens when these boundaries aren't in place and your standards haven't ever been developed? Well, you begin to let any Joe Blow enter your life, your body, and your mind. And even when you know you deserve better, sometimes you still fail to love yourself enough to demand better, granting unqualified access to your emotions and relinquishing any control you once had to someone who can't even fathom the weight of your worth.

> *Do not give dogs what is sacred; do not throw your pearls to pigs. If you do, they may trample them under their feet, and turn and tear you to pieces.*
>
> Matthew 7:6

Ladies, mutilating yourself because you don't know how to deal with the pain of an absent father is not healing. Healing is redirecting that pain in ways that lift you up, not tear you down. Take these steps to begin the healing process and begin to unveil your true identity…

RECLAIM YOUR VALUE!

Take Action:

Step 1: Be So Honest With Yourself It Hurts

Acknowledge the hurt! Be clear about every aspect of your pain, how you feel, why it hurts, who hurt you, and why it's been so challenging for you to move past it. This is the healing! Be truthful of what you've done to compensate the pain or hide it, and let it go! Cry it out, pray it out, or scream it out, but let it all out in a way you haven't before and KEEP IT OUT!

Step 2: Rewrite Your Story

This is the dealing! Stop reliving your past repeatedly, telling everything he didn't do, and creating this "Woe Is Me" story line. Get uncomfortable sharing your story at length and condense it to simple truths that will allow you to change your role from the victim to the victor and begin to take responsibility for where you are and your future.

Step 3: Forgive Yourself

Often as a result of what others have done to us or said to us, we will buy into it and begin to speak those same negatives into our lives. So, we not only have to forgive our fathers for not being present, but we also have to forgive ourselves for ignorantly believing all the things we concluded about ourselves for being a Fatherless Daughter. It's simply not true!

Mantra Moment

- I am beautiful
- I am worthy of a healthy, trusting and loving relationship with a man
- My standards are a direct reflection of my worth and I'm sticking to them
- I am valuable

When to use: If you begin to question your worth and start internalizing the negative self-talk brought on by others who have hurt you. Or when you just need a reminder of who you are and what you deserve. Recite these mantras every morning when you wake and every night before you sleep for seven days.

4

PICKED OUT OF THE CROWD

Why are you trying so hard to fit in when you were born to stand out?
- Ian Wallace

As mentioned earlier in the book, we live in a world of comparison. As women, we often do this much more than men, whether it's regarding a job, a relationship, the frame of our bodies or the shade of our skin. We begin to feel like we have to compete with one another to be recognized as being better, or simply enough. Competition leads to envy and envy leads to insecurity—and it all begins with one single moment of feeling inferior. Well, for my fellow chocolate-skinned sister, who we'll refer to as *Picked Out of the Crowd,* that moment for her centered around the dark skin girl complex, that is still very much relevant today, and being beat down verbally by society and sometimes even family members.

You're about to read her story because most of us have battled with the feeling of needing to conform to other members of a group, societal pressures, or the opinions of others, and even the feeling of having to live up to some false standard of being. The desire to "fit in" in order to be accepted is one that many have tried to suppress until we have that moment of clarity, an awakening if you will, that challenges that desire and expands our perspective.

> *Many of us suffer from this split between who we are and who we present to the world in order to be accepted, but we're not letting ourselves be known, and this kind of incongruent living is soul-sucking.*
>
> - Brené Brown

I love this quote from Brené Brown because we so desperately want to belong to something, without understanding that fitting in is not belonging, and that belonging is being fully accepted as you are...being able to be present as your authentic, vulnerable, and imperfect self amongst any group of people and be okay!

As a child, *Picked Out of the Crowd* dealt with the cruelty of her peers judging her and name calling because of the shade of her skin. They would often use terms like burnt, black, crispy and skillet to describe her. Colorism at its best, a practice of discrimination by which those with lighter skin are treated more favorably than those with darker skin! She also endured the impact of hurtful statements from her family that still dance with her thoughts and linger in her mind. As if callousness in her immediate world wasn't enough, the world at large and the media only validated the derogatory labels, ignorantly given her by family and peers, and her feelings of unworthiness. Dark complexioned women who looked like her with natural hair, full lips and figures were absent from the big screen, major TV roles, and magazine covers. They weren't highlighted and praised as many are today so that she could have another source of influence confirming that her black was in fact beautiful. Enduring this for the majority of her childhood and adolescent life was certainly challenging. Still today, like anyone else in the ring fighting to overcome an undesirable experience, it's a daily journey. Trying to get over the fact that she doesn't have to look a certain way, speak a certain way, or dress a certain way to get a stamp of approval is a tough process, but she found that the rewards for hanging in there, round for round, were greater.

It wasn't until she went to college, started coming into her own and was actually *Picked Out of the Crowd* by a guy who would later become her boyfriend, that she had that Aha moment and said, "Wow, somebody notices me! Maybe I am attractive; maybe I am someone to be *Picked Out of the Crowd* from all the other women… Maybe!"

A defense mechanism isn't something you can get rid of overnight or by simply turning off a switch, but to begin the process of filtering it out, it starts with acknowledgement. Acknowledging that this is something you're challenged with and you're not happy about it; it's not the person you want to be. From there, you have to accept and embrace the diversity of the human race. We are all very different, with different skills, abilities, and looks. It's the negative self-talk that gets us! And we've got to take control of it while also having the courage to shield ourselves from the critical views of others!

Just like *Picked Out of The Crowd,* I would also be happily surprised when someone picked me, called me beautiful or endorsed my abilities. If someone paid me a compliment, my response would unequivocally be "Really? You think so?" I would then go on to ask more questions concerning whatever it was they praised me for so that I could hear more of how great they thought I was. So sad, but so true! I would hang on to their every word because at that time I lived by the approval of others. And even when I finally got to the point where my peers and family would say things that I longed to hear, I would find some way to minimalize it by turning the focus on them—uplifting them because for some reason I felt that if they praised me it would somehow make them feel less, but in actuality that was my issue. So, in fact, I was the worst at taking compliments because deep down inside I didn't believe it myself. And what a huge awakening moment that was for me when I figured that out!

When we begin to love and value ourselves, we can offer so much more to the world and extend that love to others as well. The moment you begin to recognize the negative self-talk that comes from a place of comparison, you will be able to put a process in place to stop it, address it, and move from a place of envy to inspiration. Envy depletes you, and at every stage of life (childhood to adolescence to adulthood) we think we'll move past it, but it will only stop when you make it stop. You can operate from a space of envy your whole life if you let yourself. It's truly an unhealthy place to be and it's up to us to manage it.

The bravest thing you can ever do is own every bit of your imperfections and your personal story. Society has created the culture of "not good enough" and unfortunately, we are all buying into it. Our stories, or imperfections, the very things that makes us us, that makes us all uniquely different is becoming diminished and replaced by airbrushed visuals on social media, music videos, and television. Who said our story had to be like everyone else's story, our beauty like someone else's beauty? Who set that standard? And why do we feel like we have to follow?

Devaluing yourself is simply a lack of gratitude for your own life, your own gifts...your own beauty. There's always going to be someone better, prettier, smarter etc., but it should never take away from everything that you are.

As women, we have to first work internally, then externally together to tear down these strongholds devaluing us and negatively influencing our children, ourselves, and our gender. I once heard someone at a conference say, "when we tear down a door that wasn't meant for us to walk through, we not only need to hold it open for the women trialing behind us, but we need to tear it off the hinges!" I liked that idea so much that I quickly jotted it down on the closest thing I could find—a napkin!

The point, though, is this: You've got to own your self-worth and not base it on the success of your kids, your ability to climb the corporate ladder, your degrees, the texture of your hair, or the color of your skin. Base your self-worth on your ability to be a good person and the gift of being happy, whole, and alive.

The hustle of worthiness stops with us, and when you feel like you're being overlooked and undervalued just know that you're just being prepared for greatness! You're experiencing a test that will encourage other women just like you through your testimony. So stay faithful, stay grateful, and stay unapologetically in love with yourself.

RECLAIM YOUR VALUE!

Mantra Moment

- I am at peace with who I am
- I am enough
- I am valuable

When to use: When you find yourself struggling with insecurity, and your self-confidence begins to suffer as a result of feeling like you need to alter who you are to be recognized by others. Write these mantras down on your favorite color post-it note, place it on your bathroom mirror and recite them as soon as you wake up each morning and before bed each night for seven days. Be sure to reflect on what they actually mean and believe it!

5

SHORT HAIR DON'T CARE

As you become more clear about who you really are, you'll be better able to decide what is best for you - the first time around.
– Oprah

It's no secret that we can be moved by the way someone makes us feel. Whether they produce a feeling within us that is good or bad, if impactful enough, it can shift our actions in a way that causes us to do more of a thing, the exact opposite of that thing or never do that thing ever again.

As women, men tend to have the power of making us respond in all of those ways, when or if we let them. Take myself for example. When I entered Hampton University (that beautiful home by the sea) as a freshman from Durham, North Carolina, I must admit I was a little culture shocked. Where I lived everyone had a fresh pair of Air Force Ones (sneakers) and butter (or wheat) Timberland boots to start the school year. At Hampton, the attire was a lot trendier and fashion forward, and for some, the heels or polished and put together look may have been a little too nice for that 8 a.m. class or the cafe, but certainly more than appropriate for a two minute walk through the student center, just in case you ran into someone that day.

Many may have been intimidated by the style difference or maybe even pressured to keep up with the Joneses, but not me — I loved it and embraced it! Now was I trying to keep up? No, but Hampton students enjoyed looking nice and I appreciated that and refined my own look because of it. And the moment I did, people began to respond to me in ways I never experienced before. I felt desired and beautiful because I was able to find my own style — clean and chic — and was confident in it! I found my lane and that was an amazing feeling that I never wanted to lose. So my behavior changed in what I feel was a positive way. I became more intentional about what I selected to wear because I liked the way I felt as a result of it, and hey, the compliments were always a plus, too! But the interesting thing is that I would later realize that it wasn't the clothes, the shoes, or the makeup that impressed, because that has no true bearing on your value, but it had everything to do with my confidence, my posture, and assertiveness!

See, when you're not self-conscious and battling control over your self-image, you're able to be completely self-assured. And as someone who found themselves in the midst of that battle before entering college, I felt it was extremely important to share with you the story of *Short Hair Don't Care*, as many have experienced self-doubt and have become self-conscious about things that were never self-inflicted, but imparted by others. Her story is a prime example of that.

Very classy and humbled, *Short Hair Don't Care,* grew up as an African American in a predominantly white environment. She never really knew people would look at her and find her attractive. She didn't look like the people around her and she didn't look like the girls at school. The boys she encountered never asked her out, so she didn't date throughout high school. However, while exploring potential colleges she received a scholarship from a historically black university that she would later visit with her dad and experience something she had never experienced before.

She said, "As I walked across this HBCU's campus heads turned looking at me. I couldn't figure out why, but I knew it was a feeling I had never experienced in my life, and that there was exactly where I was going to school!" We all shared a laugh out loud and a few "I know that's right!" because we could imagine doing the same thing in that situation!

When *Short Hair Don't Care* began college it was a really different experience for her because she was judged based off who people thought she was, for the texture of her hair, her lighter skin and even how she spoke. She described this experience as being "bizarre," especially as a freshman hearing all of these things others presumed about her that she had never heard before. In high school, she had teachers who said things like "You're very articulate," or "You're very smart." That wasn't offensive at the time because she didn't any context; she just thought "They know I'm smart!" and never thought anything else about it. So this made her undergrad experience a very challenging one, trying to sort out all of this data and make sense of it in reference to figuring out who she was.

She was never a girl who cared much about the styling of her hair and was fine just wearing a painter's cap, keeping it braided or up in a bun. She started to date this guy who was a jock—a great looking guy—and they really had a lot of fun together. One day she and her girlfriends decided to get haircuts prior to going to a Yard (campus) party and she hadn't seen her boyfriend all day. She was so excited to show off her new look. It was the shortest she had ever cut her hair, but she loved it! She finally saw him and his response was: "You have totally ruined the whole LL complex. Baby, we're done!" ("LL complex" referring to light skin, long hair—the color complex in the black community that has been perpetuated for centuries. It assumes that if you had light skin and long hair you were the epitome of beauty.) So, he immediately broke up with her right there on the spot in the middle of the party because all of her pretty long hair no longer existed.

Talking about things that stay in your mind forever, *Short Hair Don't Care* described this as a defining moment in her life. It gave her something else to be self-conscious about that she had never been self-conscious about before. Her hair had never created an issue that she couldn't dismiss until that moment. Prior, it had to do with women being envious of her because of its wavy texture, something she couldn't control and that had everything to do with her genes. Now, the judgement was concerning its length as if it defined her beauty or determined her value. This experience was truly devastating, and would be for anyone who received that type of reaction to something they thought was cool and had the prerogative to do.

What this experience did to *Short Hair Don't Care,* was made her run back to her comfort zones, shift her focus, and behavior and come up with what she thought were more important things to channel her energy. Sound familiar? So, for her, for a lot of years following that day she went back to who she was before ever becoming a college student. It became about her mind and nothing to do with what her body looked like or what her hair looked like, it was about building her life and her career and exploring what her mind could do for her. She felt great about herself and never felt pressure to conform, so she thought.

Short Hair Don't Care would later marry. She was excited and thought she knew what marriage meant, thought it was going to be great! But instead of the happily ever after she envisioned, her marriage forced her to face a truth she wasn't aware of, teaching her major lessons of how she thought she had good self-esteem and valued herself; she thought she understood her worth. Isn't it amazing how we can go through life thinking one thing while being blind to reality?

She found herself putting up with a lot of bad stuff within her relationship and discovered that she wasn't valuing herself the way she should because she allowed a lot of things that weren't okay to be okay, like raising her daughter to think that the way her father treated her mother was an okay way for a woman to treated or live, that when you know things aren't right within your relationship, and you're not being treated with the respect and love you deserve you don't brush it under the rug and just deal. She decided that it wasn't selfish to show her little girl what and who a woman is supposed to be, and that it also wasn't selfish to remove her son from an environment that wasn't conducive to showing him who a man was supposed to be to a woman. *Short Hair Don't Care* ended her marriage, not only because she deserved better, but because her children deserved better. She realized that it wasn't selfish to say to herself: "you deserve more," so she took responsibility of the picture she was painting and made a conscious effort to clean the canvas.

Now, having adolescents who were becoming very self-conscious of what they looked like and also very aware of how men looked at their now single mother, she was forced to change her perspective a bit and not completely loose concentration on her physical appearance. Although *Short Hair Don't Care* wasn't moved that men would take notice when she would add a little color to her lips or style her hair, her daughter, who was watching her every move, was now at a stage where she was trying to figure all this out for herself. So instead of completely avoiding it, she wanted to teach her daughter another lesson by example to care about what you look like, not to the extent of pleasing others, but to please yourself! If you want to wear makeup or wear nothing but lip gloss, go for it! If you want to cut your hair, don't be afraid! She never wanted her to feel pressured to do anything more or less than she desired in order to get the attention of a man, keep one or feel beautiful. She had already learned that lesson…

What incredible life lessons she's epitomizing for her daughter and son: the importance of not measuring yourself by the criteria of other people. The importance of being confident in who you are and not allowing anyone to shame you into being something you're not. The importance of knowing when you're not getting what you deserve and having the ability to position yourself to invite "the more" in your life and relationships that you're worth having.

RECLAIM YOUR VALUE!

Mantra Moment

- What others say is a reflection of them, not me
- No one can make me feel unworthy without my permission
- I am valuable

When to use: Use this when you feel criticized about your abilities, your relationships (or the lack thereof), how you dress, where you live, or your weight, to protect your confidence and avoid self-loathing. Write these mantras down on your favorite color sticky note and place it on your bathroom mirror. Recite these mantras every morning when you wake and every night before sleep for seven days.

6

THE POWER OF BEAUTY

Everything that we do, how we view ourselves, how we engage with others and how we identify ourselves with the world begins with our thoughts.
– Dominique Clark

A woman who knows her value has complete authority over her thoughts! She's mastered the ability to be completely aware of the point of views that she's allowed to enter her mind, both positive and negative, those that she her herself have originated and those that have been introduced to her by outside sources. She's learned how to train her mind and understands that what you think is what you get!

The challenge is that once we've developed a certain way of thinking about ourselves, it's hard to imagine that we can be anyone else or even change that perception. Think about it: these ideas we have of ourselves that we've been introduced to have subconsciously turned into unshakable beliefs, and so we ask ourselves "Can I really change?" "Can I be someone I never believed I was capable of being?" "Can I be the person I was understood or assumed to be?"

This next story is about a fearless woman we'll call *The Power of Beauty*, who decided to change the way she thought in order to save her life. Do you know that what and who you allow to influence your mind has the power to kill you or breathe life into you? What I'm about to share with you is so important and may be the pivot to you guarding your thoughts.

Early on in life, *The Power of Beauty* was influenced by her mother dressing her up in really pretty black patent leather shoes and frilly socks, bows in her hair, and sitting her on the front porch like a doll to be admired. She was told to sit on the front porch and not get up or get dirty. While she watched the other neighborhood kids play and shout out questions to her like "You can't come out and play?" she would reply with an annoyed "no!" because she was expected to sit down and be pretty. It was there that she would learn the magnitude of beauty. From always having to stay clean and put together when she was a child, as an adult, she would never leave her home without making herself up and looking above average, and as a result of that she says she's very vain, something she shared has always worked against her because she viewed her beauty as power.

The next thing she would share with the group would bring tears to her eyes and ours as she spoke about her fifteen years as a crack addict and how it affected her relationships and life. Her beauty landed herself in a position where she was married to a drug dealer and in an abusive relationship that she wanted out of, but didn't know how to escape. She began to see another man outside of her marriage. When her husband found out about her extra marital affairs, he beat her physically and emotionally almost to her death, breaking her shoulder and collar bone. She said that if she hadn't had enough strength to call out her son's name who was in an adjacent room she probably wouldn't be alive today to share her story.

She managed to call the police during the incident and her husband exited their house and her life before the authorities could even show up. The guy she was dating and continued to be in a relationship with for the following ten years, she called her "saving grace," because he protected her and her son by manning their house and sitting on the front porch so that she could have enough peace of mind to be a mother to her son.

Now happily drug free and thankful for her sobriety (over seventeen years now) she has peace of mind and she's disconnected from an underpowered outlook and fully capable of really loving herself in a way that allows her true value to shine—not her beauty, but her ability to be strong in relationships with men and God and to support and uplift other women. The Power of Beauty couldn't deny God and his presence in her life and was appreciative of her daily relationship with him. Today she knows who she is and whose she is (meaning God), and she has her sharpened skill of total awareness to thank for that.

Romans 12:2 states "...be transformed by the renewal of your mind..." This Bible verse tells us that yes, we can change, and in order to see that change manifest in our lives or our relationships with self and others we must first renew our mind. To be transformed and renew your mind there's a process of conversion that has to take place, by way of inserting and deleting. Inserting good by introducing your mind to fresh and positive ideas and perceptions, and deleting the bad. We have to find a replacement of the self-inflicted damage, the poor relationships we've formed, destructive activities we're involved in, and the negative channels we allow to subconsciously feed us.

Start With You

There's never a better starting point than with yourself! Beginning with you is often an eye opening experience to all the other change agents (good or bad) that's influencing your mind. Another reason why beginning with yourself is so important is that you're the only person who can filter what enters and resides in your mind. Our personal thoughts and opinions of ourselves are crucial, but the most empowering factor about that—even though most fail to realize it, acknowledge it or lack a willingness to take action—is that we have control over every one of them! Looking back, it amazes me how much I entertained the crazy thoughts that once popped in my head; some I thoughtlessly dwelled upon and others I allowed to fester and internalized because I didn't know any better and was silly enough to believe them.

I know that you have experienced this too, we all have! But the turning point is when we begin to choose what thoughts we implant into our minds, and choose what realities those thoughts become.

Acknowledge & Create Awareness of Your Thoughts

It amazes me how often we allow hurt to have a magnetic grip on our heart. We'll find ourselves so inundated with emotions that it shades our vision and creates an inability to gain clarity and receive constructive disruptions to release us from its gravity. Something always brings us back, right? And without any physical effort we're bound, mentally held captive by our own insecurities, life challenges or simply failure to acknowledge that we deserve greater.

So, how do we create barriers against this commonality, you ask? I'll tell you. By embracing one of the most powerful abilities we all have: becoming self-aware. By creating awareness and acknowledging your thoughts, you are immediately able to act consciously instead of reacting to people and events. You'll be able to redirect your negative thoughts and emphasize positive ones and finally, you'll be able to have more meaningful experiences and an enjoyable life by behaving positively instead of creating additional obstacles for yourself.

Once you have complete awareness, and can effectively filter what enters your mind and life, you'll be able to detach yourself from that magnetic grip and have peace!

Now, I'm a stickler for having peace of mind. It's a daily goal of mine, because there's nothing like it! No matter the daily challenges, if we give control of that precious gift (peace of mind) to someone else we can only blame ourselves. When I realized this and internalized it, an immediate mind shift took place. I developed a spirt of gratitude and immense appreciation simply because God is where I am and where I'm going, and there's nothing that can bring peace of mind more than that one fact alone.

A huge part of training your mind and altering your thoughts is giving yourself permission to change them. Without the constraints of societal, familial or all the other outside pressures and expectations, we have to give ourselves permission to be happy and allow our minds to be a safe space for our thoughts to enter and produce positive emotions. Once you've given yourself the go-ahead to change, to follow through you need to develop a system!

Developing a system begins with making a choice and a daily effort to get to the more present us, the woman who understands her being today and embraces the individualistic power she holds because of it, the woman who is happy within because she is, and will only be, defined by the standards she impresses upon herself.

RECLAIM YOUR VALUE!

Take Action:

1. Stop comparing yourself to other people. Be proud of your uniqueness and embrace it! Appreciate your journey and understand that God has purposely planted you in this space, and in this season for a reason intended for your good.

2. Love yourself even through your mistakes. Embrace the good and the bad, and understand that life is about growing. We grow when we learn and we learn through our mistakes.

3. Don't be stagnant! Continue to move toward something that motivates you and write down your progress.

4. Maintain a fresh and positive perspective by reciting your favorite mantras or life quotes daily.

_____

_____

_____

_____

7

THINK HAPPY THOUGHTS!

Most people are about as happy as they make up their minds to be.
– Abraham Lincoln

Have you ever thought that you needed to do something extraordinary or be someone amazingly special to experience true happiness? Ask yourself this and write your response in the space below: What is it that you feel you need to do or be in order to have the right to be happy? I'm looking for a primitive, gut answer here, not an elegant answer from your head.

You may have written something like: "I have to have a lot of money in the bank," "I have to be married," "I must be at the height of my career," "I have to look at certain way" or maybe even "I don't have the right to be happy."

Your answer should tell you exactly where your happiness is tied to and where you're trying to conform to an ideal. If your happy thoughts are tied to obtaining a degree, you'll believe that you must succeed at getting into school, completing your degree and being recognized for your academic achievement in order to be happy. And that's simply not true. Life happens, and sometimes we experience things that prevent us from checking all the items on our goal list, but that doesn't mean we have to be miserable as a result of it and allow negative thoughts to consume our minds, misleading our perspective and naively disturbing other areas of our lives.

Happiness is not something we have to earn the right to get, it's not required that we have to be perfect or untainted to have access. It's a choice, and we have the right to it when we decide to make a conscious change in the negative thoughts we've become enslaved to. We have to train our minds to think happy thoughts, because what you think is what you get, and what you get is a direct reflection of the beliefs you house in your mind, and if I even need to say it, a reflection of how valuable you think you are.

To think happy thoughts is a learned trait. We can improve how positively we see ourselves by choosing what aspects of us, our world, and the people in it to focus our attention on. And let me tell you, the benefits of such an effort are life changing! So how do you disturb this negative pattern of thinking and develop a happier point of view?

RECLAIM YOUR VALUE!

Take Action:

1. Think Optimistically! Thinking optimistically creates an attitude of hopefulness and a confidence about yourself and your future. It is proactively striving in the face of naysayers or your own limiting beliefs because of the faith you have at obtaining the desires of your heart.

2. Think on Purpose! Choose your thoughts, don't let them choose you! When you allow your mind to wander on its own, you give poor thoughts an opportunity to walk. Aim your thoughts towards the things that matter most in your life and fill your mind with amazing ideas that you can creatively grow.

3. Think Funny! Yes, that's right. Find something to laugh about. Developing a good sense of humor is essential to happiness. It's important to be able to find humor in life's challenges and not take yourself too seriously.

4. Think Higher! Think elevated thoughts of love graciousness, gratitude, humility and trust instead of pride, fear, greed, condemnation and judgment! And learn to see the best in you and others, wish the best for you and others, and think the best about you and about others.

Mantra Moment

- What's important to ME now is _____ (one word)
- I am Valuable

When to use: Use this when you start comparing yourself to others or start doubting your choices based on something outside of you and even those that you can control. It's also great for those self-critical moments that can leave you feeling powerless.

8

YOU, MY DEAR, ARE POWERFUL

The moment anyone tries to demean or degrade you in any way, you have to know how great you are. Nobody would bother to beat you down if you were not a threat.
- Cicely Tyson

YOU, my dear are very powerful! Women are powerful! So much impact in only three words and the perfect way to start this chapter and begin to end this book. I remember being home after the birth of my second child engulfed in what many call a traditional woman's work: cooking dinner, managing the kids (nursing my newborn with my left hand while simultaneously swatting my two year old's fingers from the hot stove, and flipping the meat so it wouldn't burn with my right), making sure the house was in order before my husband came home, live streaming a Marketing course while earning my MBA and creating my company's agenda for the following day in my head. Multitasking at its best! During this time, my husband was working 12-hour days, between three jobs, Monday through Monday. I would long for the hour he would come home each night so that I could have a little relief from feeling like a single parent, but I quickly realized that there's no such thing as complete relief as a woman. Our work is never done and we always have to be "on." Taking a full shower became a luxury and "me time" became the minimal hours of sleep I was able to get at night or the extended time I would sit in the car while in the driveway after running an errand.

"To whom much is given, much is required." I didn't realize how true this statement was until I really sat down and ran down the list of all the words that can describe a woman: Women are mothers, wives, a source of nourishment, sisters, friends, emotional pillows, teachers, "baby, what tie should I wear?" prayer warriors, birthers of life, thinkers, influencers, pleasure, homemakers, "What's for dinner?" molly maids, presidents of the PTA, "mommy can I," a GPS and the list goes on...Ladies, you are uniquely valuable, an asset to anyone who encounters you and a medal of honor to anyone who gets the opportunity to date or marry you.

Now that you've done the work, it's time to unveil what you now realize makes you powerful and valuable as a woman. It's time to relish and believe in that inner uniqueness that's a precious rarity like rubies.

And so I ask you, would you now say that you really know who you are? I ask this question not to get an immediate response, but for you to actually take time to reflect on the things, qualities and values you own that make you, you! Most of us don't, and until now, most of us haven't. For those just jumping on the She's Valuable bandwagon, when you're preparing yourself to do this keep in mind that the prerequisite for defining who you are does not include a comparison to other women, however, it does include a comparison of who you were to who you see yourself becoming!

See, we are naturally hardwired to define and compare. We've been taught that in order to label something we are to compare it to similar and dissimilar things before concluding what that thing actually is. For instance, my oldest daughter who is three and the light of my world, is the ultimate juice lover! She wants juice with her breakfast, with her lunch and definitely with dinner! She also expects juice while riding in the car, watching TV and while lying in bed at night! The very moment we try to sneak in milk she drops her cup and says "I want juice mommy! Juice, please!" She immediately distinguishes a difference based off the way it looks, and if I can manage to get her to take a sip, the taste makes it really obvious. It's completely ridiculous that her dad and I have created this adorable juice monster! But even at a young age, toddlers are able to define what something is by comparing it to what it's not.

As you gather your thoughts and all your discoveries from your reflections remember that your value, your worth is not attached to your ability to bear children, or to your achievements or degrees. It's not attached to your body or any superficial qualities or attributes. It's not based on a man loving you or being present in your life and it's not determined by your ability to blend in with the crowd.

When you think you're over something until something similar appears and uncovers old wounds, don't be dismayed! Be aware of your feelings and honor them, and begin to shift your thoughts to your power and your strength.

Let go of the need to be wanted and fought for, and stop questioning if others see what you see in yourself. No fight is necessary when it's clear to the right person that you are enough. They'll see the greatness in you without you even having to speak it.

Understand that we are all human and will make mistakes, but when the person you thought could do no wrong or harm you in anyway, suddenly fails you, don't lose trust in everyone else.

As you go into this next RECLAIM YOUR VALUE exercise, remember to replace your negative thoughts with high quality thoughts—that's where it starts.

So, as we begin to wrap things up I want you to know your unique value proposition. If you're an entrepreneur or someone in the business world, when you hear the words *unique value proposition,* a startup business, or product probably comes to mind. Now, I'm sure you're thinking *what does this have to do with me realizing my worth as a woman?* Where is Dominique going with this? Let me explain…

According to Forbes.com, a value proposition is a **positioning statement that explains what benefit you provide for who and how you do it uniquely well.** It describes your target buyer, the problem you solve, and why you're distinctly better than the alternatives. So, what's your positioning statement?

First, start by listing all the benefits you provide those around you. If you want to create your unique value proposition in terms of relationships, list what benefits you'll be able to provide a man within a relationship.

_____

_____

Second, think about what separates you from all the other women in the world, or to make it simpler, the women in your immediate circle. Write this distinction down.

_____

_____

Third, think Minimal Viable Product! At minimum, what makes you great? List your statement below:

_____

_____

_____

_____

> *After all those years as a woman hearing 'not thin enough, not pretty enough, not smart enough, not this enough, not that enough,' almost overnight I woke up one morning and thought, "I'm enough."*
>
> -Anna Quindlen

9

SHE'S VALUABLE
(BUT DOES HE KNOW IT?)

Understand that you date at the level of your self-esteem, you love at the level in which you love yourself, and you attract whom you truly believe you deserve. The common denominator is you.
– Dominique Clark

S o, why does the content of this book matter? How does living in your true value and presenting the next best version of yourself help you to win in love and dating?

When you know your worth, you create a realm of tailored possibilities for yourself, and as a Matchmaker, of course I couldn't end this book without addressing the possibility of love—the possibility of a real, happy and lasting relationship happening to you now that you're using language like "I'm worthy" and "I deserve" and started distancing yourself from those with a "struggle" mindset.

Complete the following phrase: I am worthy of a healthy, lasting relationship because...

_____

_____

_____

_____

Before you ever think about dating, you need to think about this: *why me?* Honestly answering this question is the ultimate prerequisite to entering a healthy relationship. Without doing the work I challenged you with throughout the course of this book, you will never attract the man you deserve because the woman you'll present will only represent the old you—the woman who is broken, weighed down with emotional baggage, has thoughts of never being enough and settles, because, let's face it, her past tells her she shouldn't dare think she was worthy of more.

So how do you bridge the gap?

Someone once asked me "What's the biggest reason why people are failing at relationships on their own, (meaning without the help of a coach and matchmaker like me)?" My response: lack of strategy. There are way too many people dating by default and it drives me insane! It really makes me want to pull all of my hair out because their expectations are so great, yet their intention to date on purpose is miniscule! How can that be? In order to be successful in life, love, or business you have to have a strategy. You need an action plan. It may seem bizarre to think that you have to have a strategy for love, but you do, and it works!

I strategized with my husband. Since our goal was to make it fifty plus years with each other, we had to have a plan on how we were going to get there. This plan included everything from how we would communicate with one another, how we would manage our finances, how we would consistently stimulate each other intimately, emotionally and spiritually, kids (and when we would have them), what involvement our extended families and friends would have in our lives, etc. Though our plan may have shifted a little over the years as our lives did, the foundation we created has been invaluable to the success of our relationship, and I'm so thankful for it.

Now, you could be thinking "what if I'm not in a relationship yet?" That's okay! You still need a strategy! Even though I was extremely young when I started seriously dating my husband (only sixteen years old) I developed an unbreakable plan for myself because I didn't take relationships lightly being a product of a single parent and refusing to continue the legacy of divorce. So, I implemented a three part action plan before approaching dating with any expectation of success, and here's what I did:

1. Be me. I had to develop the mentality that if someone wanted to be with me they would accept me wholeheartedly for who I was (of course after I had done the same first), because who I was mattered.

2. Value and protect myself. I had to completely value myself, protect myself, and reserve all of me for someone

who was worthy, someone who would be willing to put the effort in to know and cherish the person I had come tolove and know.

3. When I got to the point when I felt READY to engage intimately with someone (sharing of my mind, body, and emotions on a deeper level), I had to ensure that it was someone that I knew without a shadow of a doubt was deserving of that, someone who knew how to handle me with care and who would respect me in every way possible when given such a precious gift.

That was my plan...a plan of knowing my worth, protecting it and engaging cautiously with potential partners. Because of that plan, I was walking in power! I was in control, and I know it's the only reason that I was able to successfully pick the right person for myself without worry of the aftermath; without worry if I was going to be devastated or puzzled with thoughts of "I really thought we had something" if the relationship didn't work. I was confident in my ability to choose well because I was confident in myself and valued my self-worth. And that's why this book matters! The quality of our relationships is tied inevitably to our level of self-worth. Because I valued myself, I could always count on engaging with men who would do the same. I understood that the relationship not working didn't speak to my worth or them not recognizing it, it spoke to our lack of compatibility (which I'll address in my next book that's specifically focused on relationships and finding lasting love).

So, what's your plan? Spend some time really thinking about an effective strategy for yourself, something simple enough that you can put in action today, but sound enough that it will allow you to attract the type of men who will value you and who actually deserve you. If you find it hard to create your own plan, adopt mine until you're able to personalize one for yourself. Write your plan down on the next page.

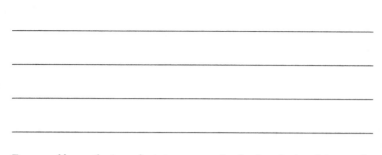

Poor self-worth is what traps us in bad relationships, what sabotages new relationships, and what causes us to feel broken when a relationship ends. Knowing your worth doesn't guarantee a happy relationship of course, but it certainly equips you with the ability to identify what you need and deserve before you ever think about entering one.

Knowing your value (or not) and how you communicate it affects your love life, so I wanted to provide you with a few examples of its impact:

When You Don't Know:

You're constantly looking for someone to "fix" you, and you make getting the relationship you desire about someone else rather than yourself.

When You Know:

You attract the person who sees you, who appreciates the love you have for yourself and wants to love you with that same magnitude or greater.

When You Don't Know:

You self-sabotage. You're subconsciously verbally and emotionally abusive to yourself while single, and in turn are abusive in that same manner to your partner and or relationship.

When You Know:

You respect yourself enough to move on from bad relationships, and realize that if it doesn't work you're not any less of a person; you were just involved with someone you weren't compatible with.

When You Don't Know:

You find yourself changing who you are or minimalizing yourself for the relationship. You feel pressured to be someone other than yourself.

When You Know:

You know you are loved and lovable and you're not desperately seeking reassurance from others. The love you have for yourself is enough, and love from others is just a bonus.

Have you ever found yourself asking God "When is true love ever going to happen for me?" I know I have, and I can name countless others too! Especially when you see your friends and family progressing in their relationships, it's so hard not to yearn for that and question when your turn is. We all anxiously want to know *when* our moment is, right? But, I'd like to challenge you to change your perspective a little and instead ask *"What is my moment?"* *"What* does true love look like for *me?"* This minor but effective shift in thinking that was impressed on me will release any pressuring timelines you or anyone else has created for yourself. It will allow you to confidently stay in your lane, on your path, and genuinely celebrate those who've achieved the relationship success that you desire. Most importantly, when you understand *what* true love looks like for you, you're able to recognize and take advantage of the right relationship opportunities and avoid what wasn't intended for you in the first place. You'll experience an immediate confidence boost and maintain a hopeful attitude towards love.

So, how do you figure out what true love looks like for you, specifically? You take a look in the mirror and really get to know the person staring back at you. You learn your weaknesses so you can identify where he should be strong, you learn your strengths so that you know where you can carry him, you learn your emotional, spiritual, physical, and financial needs so that you can identify his ability to fulfil them. And needless to say, you learn your value so that without question you can confirm his knowledge of that by the way he protects you, affirms you, publicly adores you and uncontrollably loves you.

When you're in tune with yourself, you'll find it extremely difficult to be paired with someone grooving to a different beat. He could be just a few seconds off count, but instead of allowing him to get you completely off rhythm too, you won't mind giving the solo of your life until you attract the man who is totally in sync with you. It's at this point that you'll recognize WHEN is far less significant than WHAT, and that true love is worth the wait, because settling is never an option for the woman who knows her worth.

Now, let's take this concept a step further. Once you've found yourself happily in a relationship with the right person, let's talk about how to maintain your self-worth and not lose yourself in a relationship.

There is nothing like having the freedom and self-confidence to be your authentic self in a relationship. Being able to express my goofy, sometimes emotional, always talkative, high energy, nail-biting-when-nervous and Beyoncé wannabe (in and outside the shower) self is like a breath of fresh air. I'm so thankful that I can now love who I am and not be afraid to share it. You have to bring the fullness of who you are to a relationship and if you can't do that, you allow important parts of you to die. That's a sure sign that you're with the wrong person. When you don't maintain your value you become nonexistent in a relationship, and so does your identity, and ladies, that's too precious to lose!

So how do you build a daily practice of maintaining your worth while in a relationship? Here are a several proven methods I use with my clients that will help you do so:

MAINTAIN YOUR VALUE!

Take Action:

1. Find validation within yourself

Knowing that you are understood and that your partner accepts your emotions and thoughts is powerful, but accepting your own internal experiences, thoughts, challenges, and feelings is even more powerful. It will allow you to empower yourself and be fully present in a relationship without constantly seeking validation from your man; doing so will only cause your relationship to suffer.

The key here is visualization! You have to visualize yourself in control, every day! Believe that you are full of everything you need (because you are!) and you'll no longer feel frustrated and empty trying to get complete fulfillment and validation from your mate.

2. Honor and communicate your needs and wants

How can you be available as your best self for your mate if you're not taking care of you? When we're in a relationship ladies, we can often forget about our own needs and desires because we make it all about him and his needs. We try so hard to keep him and maintain his interest that we forget we are also worthy to be kept.

You have to get familiar with your needs by first asking yourself what they are. Then you need to get comfortable communicating those needs. Doing so does not make you a selfish person or a burden. You're actually operating out of self-love, and as a result, you begin to create a mutually respectful space where both you and your man can openly express your needs. You'll find that your relationship will have more love, trust, and transparency.

3. Do something every day for you, showing that you love and honor yourself

It's so important not to shrink yourself while in a relationship. You have to remember to always maintain the identity you had prior to your mate. Don't resist your dreams or career to boost your man's ego or feelings; you can have a relationship and success at the same time (I'm proof!). Don't sever ties with your friends or other important relationships because his social circle may be small; you don't want to create an unhealthy dependency or lose others that you love.

Instead, create a healthy balance of time away from your partner with your friends and have that rejuvenating girl time that we all need, right? Hang on to your own personal interests and hobbies and continue to do them. Give yourself the quiet time you need to finish that book or write that blog, give yourself alone time to buy that dress or just get your nails done. Enjoy the simple pleasures of life—you always have to maintain your personal happiness! Believe it or not, your relationship depends on that.

Understand that you date at the level of your self-esteem, you love at the level in which you love yourself, and you attract who you truly believe you deserve. The common denominator is you. YOU ARE VALUABLE! Act accordingly!

_____

_____

Reclaim Your Value
30 DAY SNATCH BACK!

Allow the next 30 days to be your best 30 days while you use these daily affirmative truths to help you snatch back your value, empower your mind and transform your self-image!

Day One

TRUTH:

I AM A STRONG WOMAN WITH GREAT COURAGE

Reflect and Respond:
Reflect on a time where you had to be brave and face the trials and tribulations of life. Recognize and praise yourself for having the tenacity to overcome. Write down all your strengths you discovered and remind yourself of them during your next challenge.

Day Two

TRUTH:

I AM A WOMAN OF INTEGRITY, BOTH IN MY HEART AND IN MY ACTIONS

Reflect and Respond:
Do you battle with being trustworthy? Are you able to be honest with yourself about your true feelings? Today empower yourself to make decisions that honor your mind, body and spirit.

Day Three

TRUTH:

I WILL NOT HOLD ON TO AN OFFENSE OR BE SPITEFUL

Reflect and Respond:
A woman of value is compassionate and forgiving. Can it be hard to be quick to forgive and quick to apologize? Absolutely! But anger and resentment are not valuable qualities. Humble yourself and show grace toward someone today. Reflect on and write down how it made you feel and their response to you doing it.

Day Four

TRUTH:

IT IS OKAY TO BE SELF-FOCUSED

Reflect and Respond:
There's a difference between being selfish and being self-focused.
Self-focused is simply prioritizing yourself in a healthy way
that allows you to be holistic and allows others to have a full
perspective on who you are. Today balance work with play by
allotting yourself a minimum of 30 minutes of uninterrupted "me
time."

Day Five

TRUTH:

I AM WISE AND MAKE FRUITFUL DECISIONS

Reflect and Respond:
Are you impatient and typically act on a whim? Or do you make
rash, emotional decisions that may feel good now? When you
understand your worth you take the time to make decisions that
will benefit you long term by logically analyzing your options
before making a choice. Write down whatever it is you're
impatiently waiting for and brainstorm the most beneficial route
to achieving it before you act or speak.

Day Six

TRUTH:

I AM KIND, THOUGHTFUL, AND UNGRUDGINGLY AVAILABLE TO THOSE IN NEED

Reflect and Respond:

Does your life have you in a space where you are too "busy" or often wait until the last minute to help others? I'm not going to lie, it's tough to concern yourself with the comfort of others while also thinking about your own, but there is no greater feeling than taking advantage of an opportunity to serve the less fortunate of those who just need a break. Be kind to someone today and without begin asked, extend a helping hand or pour into their life without expecting anything in return.

Day Seven

TRUTH:

I TAKE PRIDE IN MY BODY, HEART, AND MIND

Reflect and Respond:
You're valuable! Although there's nothing wrong with wearing sweats and a messy bun every now and then, keep yourself up and present yourself accordingly. You need to celebrate your womanhood! Today, clean yourself up, dress up, and remind yourself and the world of the gem it has while taking joy in your beauty, both inside and out!

Day Eight

TRUTH:

WHEN I SPEAK, I HAVE SOMETHING WORTHWHILE TO SAY, AND I ALWAYS SAY IT KINDLY

Reflect and Respond:

Do you add value to a conversation? Are you cutting people down or building them up? You have to learn the power of your words! They should be sweet like honey and filled with wisdom. Today, be intentional about your choice of words. Be slow to speak, the first to listen, and the last to say something unkind.

Day Nine

TRUTH:

MY BEAUTY IS NOT JUST SKIN DEEP, IT REACHES THE SOUL

Reflect and Respond:
Do you find yourself getting caught up in the latest trends or society's expectations of you? Turning heads with your physical attributes is great, but one day you will be old and grey. Don't allow your charm to outweigh your substance! Today, seek improvement, growth and contentment—the result of these things will never fade.

Day Ten

TRUTH:

REFLECT ON YOUR GROWTH AND PRAISE YOURSELF FOR LOVING YOU ENOUGH TO CHANGE AND EXPRESS YOUR TRUE VALUE!

Day Eleven

TRUTH:

THERE IS NO ONE ELSE ON THE PLANET LIKE ME, AND THERE NEVER WILL BE

Reflect and Respond:
Aren't you glad you were made an original and not a coy? To be a one-of-a-kind means the world is fortunate to have you, so don't underestimate your presence and your unique ability to be fantastically you! You are loved and admired more than you'll ever know.

Today, resist the urge to compare yourself to others. Reflect on all your matchless qualities and write them down.

Day Twelve

TRUTH:

I DESERVE EVERYTHING GOOD
THAT COMES MY WAY

Reflect and Respond:
Think about the last time something really amazing happened
to you. Did you feel unqualified for that promotion? Or not
good enough to receive that praise or recognition? Know that
a valuable woman is worthy of favor, in fact, it flocks to her
without cause. Today, be grateful for all the wonderful things in
your life and forgive yourself for ever feeling underserving.

Day Thirteen

TRUTH:

I SURROUND MYSELF WITH GOOD PEOPLE WHO MAKE POSITIVE DEPOSITS IN MY LIFE

Reflect and Respond:

Who's in your circle? Do you associate yourself with negative people who depreciate your worth? Do they take advantage of your generosity and are only looking to make a withdrawal? We don't make it in this world alone, so make sure those with you are honest and loving. Make a list of the five people you spend the most time with. Ask yourself are they your supporters or your doubters? Do they value themselves? Do they value you? Do they criticize you or show you ways to improve? Do they inspire you? Reflect on this list then ask yourself is it time to get a new circle?

Day Fourteen

TRUTH:

I AM HAPPY

Reflect and Respond:
Think back to a time when you were immensely happy. Where were you, who was around, what were you doing? Real happiness comes from knowing who you are and being the best that you can be; you have the right to it! Today, write down all the healthy things that make you happy, do at least one today and every day!

Day Fifteen

TRUTH:

I AM IN CONTROL OF MY OWN THOUGHTS

Reflect and Respond:
It's so easy to respond to all the wrong in our lives, but I challenge you to embrace what is good in your life and let go of the rest! Maintaining a positive mindset is key in filtering out unfavorable thoughts. A valuable woman values her mind by guarding who and what she allows to contribute to it. Today, take responsibility and ownership of your thoughts. Any negative self-talk or opinions from others check immediately at the door and replace them with something affirmative.

Day Sixteen

TRUTH:

I TRUST MYSELF

Reflect and Respond:
Do you trust yourself enough? A lack of faith in yourself is
impeding the wealth, love, freedom and impact you want to
create. So, if you spend a lot of time regretting things you've done
or decisions you've made, you don't trust yourself. If you weren't
always trustworthy, you don't trust yourself. Compile a list of
all the ways you do trust yourself and give yourself permission
to take pride in them. This will give you a hefty boost to your self-
confidence and subsequently your self-trust.

Day Seventeen

TRUTH:

I AM FREE TO LAUGH AND ENJOY ALL LIFE HAS TO OFFER

Reflect and Respond:

When was the last time you had a really good laugh? Are you giving yourself a fair chance at living a joyous life? Don't take yourself or life so seriously that you allow yourself or others to prevent you from relishing in all life's little funny moments. Today, care enough about yourself to laugh out loud without fear of the future. Being able to laugh is a sign of an optimistic personality and sense of humor, and it just simply puts you in a good mood.

Day Eighteen

TRUTH:

I AM NOT PERFECT, AND THAT'S OKAY

Reflect and Respond:
Do you feel like you have to have it all together all the time?
DON'T! Nobody does! Remember all that glitters isn't gold.
People appreciate real people, people who aren't afraid to show
their flaws and admit that they are only human. Today, stop
reaching for perfection. If you make a mistake, that's okay! Take
responsibility and keep it moving. Experience a challenging
situation? Remember life is full of ups and downs, but there is
always light at the end of the tunnel.

Day Nineteen

TRUTH:

I CAN HAVE A STANDARD AND STILL WIN

Reflect and Respond:
Do you have standards in terms of intimate relationships? I mean have you really taken the time to consider and set a reasonable bar for men to reach? Devaluing yourself because you think you'll have a better chance at having a relationship is a bad idea. Having a standard means you understand your worth and you deserve someone that sees and appreciates that. Write down five reasonable standards that a man must reach to have access to your heart, mind and body. Then actually apply these standards in order to see the increase you want in your life, relationships, and friendships.

Day Twenty

TRUTH:

REFLECT ON YOUR GROWTH AND PRAISE YOURSELF FOR LOVING YOU ENOUGH TO CHANGE AND EXPRESS YOUR TRUE VALUE!

Day Twenty-One

TRUTH:

I AM WORTH IT!
ALWAYS WAS, AND ALWAYS WILL BE!

Reflect and Respond:
Let's keep this one short and sweet: validation is for parking, not you! Recite today's truth seven times throughout the day.

Day Twenty-Two

TRUTH:

I AM NOT FOR EVERYONE!

Reflect and Respond:

Have you ever found yourself down because a person or group didn't approve of you? The world is filled with people that no matter what you do just won't like you, and that's okay! Don't waste your precious time or gifts trying to convince someone of your value. They may never understand it, they may never believe it, leaving you broken trying to heal because they never received it. Identify and stay clear of the people to whom you've had to prove your worth. When you understand your value, the idea of swaying others to accept who you are is no longer worth entertaining.

Day Twenty-Three

TRUTH:

I AM WORTHY OF A HEALTHY, TRUSTING AND LOVING RELATIONSHIP WITH A MAN

Reflect and Respond:

Do you feel that you need to prove yourself worthy of real love? Somewhere along the way, we learned to believe we need to prove something. We have traveled so far from ourselves that it's no wonder that we've found ourselves alone and questioning our worth. Real men want the real you! So, if it's a healthy, trusting, and loving relationship that you want, be honest with yourself and realize there is no shame in being upfront about and owning the desires of your heart. Today, reflect on the things that's causing you to attract unhealthy men and relationships. Then stop it!

Day Twenty-Four

TRUTH:

I AM HEALED FROM MY PAST
AND IT DOESN'T DEFINE ME

Reflect and Respond:

Are you hanging on to emotional baggage in your mind and body that you need to release from your past? Are there triggers that instantly remind you of the hurt? Stored emotions and painful memories are a huge obstacle, but learning to acknowledge and deal with them head on is what's going to create the balance you desire and give you the ability to move on. Today, write down every past issue that's still lingering in your heart and consuming your mind. Understand that they won't be released without forgiveness, then proceed to forgive the person responsible and forgive yourself for allowing it to derail you.

Day Twenty-Five

TRUTH:

I POSSESS TOTAL CONFIDENCE

Reflect and Respond:
Lets face it; a woman without confidence is a woman unknowledgeable of her worth. I have noticed a lack of total confidence of almost epidemic proportions in women, and it simply shouldn't be! The key to generating total confidence is through identification and purposeful, daily applications of your core values. Today, take time to reflect on and establish your core values. Write them down, ingrain them in your heart, and never sway from them.

Day Twenty-Six

TRUTH:

I AM A WOMAN, AND I AM POWERFUL

Reflect and Respond:

There is no force more powerful than a woman who knows her worth. Do you understand the magnitude of your power? From the biological ability to birth life, to the ability to be strong yet gentle, educated yet humble, fierce yet compassionate, passionate yet rational, disciplined yet free and above all an influencer of all, my sister it doesn't get more powerful than that! Today reflect on what you think is your own power, wear it on your chest and never forget it.

Day Twenty-Seven

TRUTH:

I SUPPORT AND EMPOWER OTHER WOMEN

Reflect and Respond:
A woman unfamiliar with her values sees the world from a place of scarcity and lack. She competes and will even tear down another in order to secure resources or a mate. Is this you? Real women help others and are not threatened by their success. The high road is always her preferred route. Today, reach out to another woman and support her in any possible way.

Day Twenty-Eight

TRUTH:

I AM SELF-AWARE

Reflect and Respond:

Self-awareness is being in tune with what's happening around you. It's proactively viewing yourself from a position of your higher self, observing your thoughts, feelings and actions, and determining if what you're observing is aligned with who you want to be. Define the beset version of yourself. Write this down. Then begin to pay attention to what you are thinking, speaking, how you're acting, feeling, reacting and what you're attracting and what you're hiding. It's time to evolve and stop behaving in a way that pulls you out of character.

Day Twenty-Nine

TRUTH:

I AM LOVED AND WORTHY OF RESPECT

Reflect and Respond:
Do you believe you are worthy of love and respect? A woman of value demands respect, but she understands that she must love and respect herself if it's to be reciprocated by others. Today, compile a list of all the things you love about yourself, then demonstrate your self-respect by holding yourself and your life in high regard daily.

Day Thirty

TRUTH:

I AM VALUABLE

Reflect and Respond:
Believe that! No explanation needed!

VALUABLE
Pledge

I AM VALUABLE. I am a woman uniquely designed and carefully created to influence a nation. My presence is necessary.

I AM VALUABLE. I own my story, but my past will not define me. My journey is an intricate testimony that will save lives. My life matters.

I AM VALUABLE. I know my worth. I am confident and proud of who I am. I treat myself with respect and value my mind, body and heart.

I AM VALUABLE. I am an attraction magnet towards positive people and positive experiences. I maintain optimism and know that things will always work out for my good.

I AM VALUABLE. I am beautiful and incomparable. My beauty spans from the depth of my knowledge to the surface of my skin. It will not be defined by the media or other parties ignorant to my magnificence.

I AM VALUABLE. I am worthy of healthy relationships. I demand the same level of respect from men that I give myself. I trust myself to choose right for me.

I AM VALUABLE. I have no desire to be accepted by anyone other than myself and God. I am enough. My existence depends on the approval of no one.

I AM VALUABLE. I pour into the lives of my sisters and female counterparts. I am a supporter of all women.

I AM VALUABLE. I am completely and wholeheartedly in love with myself. I am lovable and loved. I choose to be happy and live my life with joy.

I AM VALUABLE. Questioning my value is never an option. I AM VALUABLE! AND I KNOW IT!

SIGNATURE

_____

DATE

_____

ABOUT THE AUTHOR

Dominique Clark is a Certified Matchmaker, Relationship Coach, and owner of DClark & Company, an exclusive agency for the busy professional in search of lasting love. She is dedicated to coaching women and men across the country on how to transform their minds, communicate their value, and transition their hearts to attract their soul mates. Driven by the promotion of self-image and understanding of self-worth, Dominique's clients applaud her ability to create meaningful dating experiences and healthy relationships. Dominique is leaving her mark in the love industry daily as a sought after coach, workshop host, and contributor/featured expert in major publications such as *SHEEN Magazine* and *Carolina Style* and television networks such as The CW and WE TV. Learn more at DClarkAndCompany.com

CPSIA information can be obtained at www.ICGtesting.com
Printed in the USA
LVOW11s0747280716

498037LV00003B/4/P